DEAL WITH IT:

The Spirit of Anger

Nori Moore

Copyright © 2021

All rights reserved.

No part of this book may be reproduced, stored in a retrieval system, or transmitted in any form or by any means, electronic, mechanical, photocopying, recording, scanning, or otherwise, without the prior written permission of the publisher.

Disclaimer

All Biblical verses are italicized and taken from the New King James Version of the Holy Bible.

Every material contained in this book is provided for educational and informational purposes only.

No responsibility can be taken for any results or outcomes resulting from the use of this material.

TABLE OF CONTENTS

INTRODUCTION 6
CHAPTER ONE 10
   MY STORY 10
CHAPTER TWO 21
   THE SPIRIT OF ANGER 21
CHAPTER THREE 27
   HOW TO IDENTIFY IT 27
CHAPTER FOUR 35
   ANGER IN THE HOME 35
CHAPTER FIVE 45
   ANGER IN THE WORKPLACE 45
CHAPTER SIX 54
   ANGER IN RELATIONSHIPS 54
CHAPTER SEVEN 62
   ANGER IN MY CALLING 62
CHAPTER EIGHT 71
   ANGER IN ABSENCE 71
CHAPTER NINE 75
   ANGER AND ME 75
CHAPTER TEN 80
   HOW TO HEAL ANGER 80
RESOURCE 88

SCRIPTURES & PRAYERS	88
CONCLUSION	98
MY REFLECTIONS	100
ABOUT THE AUTHOR	105
NORI MOORE	105

INTRODUCTION

"He who is slow to anger is better than the mighty, and he who rules his spirit than he who takes a city." - **Proverbs 16:32**

It has been a long time coming, but here we are, ready to **DEAL WITH IT.** That is how we and so many others have viewed this hideous monster in our life; as an IT. For far too long, the Spirit of Anger has gone unaddressed. We have tried to do life as if IT were not there, tormenting, controlling, shaming, and destroying us.

The truth of the matter is, the Spirit of Anger has reared its ugly head way too many times in our families, relationships, careers, and ministries. You and I have been fighting a vicious battle known only to a few and misunderstood by many. Like a thief that comes in the night, the Spirit of Anger has come to steal, kill, and destroy. We have personally experienced its destructive powers in our life up-close and far too frequently. Clearly, it was sent to rob us of our God-given peace and God-ordained happiness.

This is why the Spirit of Anger must be identified and quickly addressed in an individual's life. It is important to understand that no gender, race, or age group is safe from such a destructive monster. We must ready ourselves to identify ITS workings in our life and have complete determination to execute a strategic plan in demolishing its very existence in our lives, family, and relationships.

Today we deal with IT. Today we make a conscious decision to slay this hideous giant in our life. We will no longer grant this monster access to our soul nor our spirit. Enough is enough. Throughout this book, I will be intentional about identifying, targeting, and demolishing the Spirit of Anger. I will share with you some of my very own experiences, methods, and victories. This book is in no way intended to provide any form of professional counseling or guidance but only a source of comfort and encouragement from one friend to another.

My intent is to help you openly acknowledge that the Spirit of Anger is real, and it has, to some degree or another, taken root in you. Confession is the prerequisite to deliverance. It is often the hardest step but necessary to the road of recovery. So much of our normalcy has been lost in the grips of our madness. Our life has become so frail. Surely this is not what we dreamed when we viewed the distance of our days.

Often the Spirit of Anger is the result of unforgiveness or some form of resentment. Confession is a step in the right direction, but then you must identify the root cause. I want you to begin to think about this as we move into the depths of this book. I want you to go back to where it all began. I would encourage you to do this time of recalling with prayer. Pray that our Lord and Savior would safely guide you back to review that traumatic moment in time. Ask him to reveal the satanic agenda that was loosed in your life to rob you of all the glorious moments and relationships He purposed for you. It is my prayer that you can gain a revelatory understanding and, in turn, a fervent tenacity to fight for your freedom. Oh yes! I did say fight. I will arm you with key artillery to ensure your victory over this hideous monster called anger.

Life does not have to continue as we have known it. It is time to face our giant! It is time to enjoy the joys of life! We will no longer lay down and allow this hideous monster to control us or our world.

I, too, had a day I decided that I would no longer be the victim but the victor. The Spirit of Anger had tormented and controlled my life for over thirty years, and I was tired of feeling defeated. I had sat back long enough and watched it sweep through my life like a ravenous wolf, destroying everything and everyone I loved. The spirit of conviction came upon me heavily. I felt it in my sleep; it sat on me throughout the day. I understood more than ever that God wanted me free more than I ever wanted to be free. That was powerful! To know it grieved Him to see me being tormented and destroyed moved me from complacency and contentment to concern. I knew something had to be done, and it had to be done quickly. As you move forward in this book, it is my prayer that you, too, will be ignited to gain victory in your life.

I will tell you what I know, heard, and saw that led me to victory. I invite you into my story....

CHAPTER ONE
MY STORY

It was one of the most joyous times of my life. You see, I was only thirteen years old. I was just starting to experience life. In my mind, nothing could go wrong. Everything was perfect. I was young and eager, yet so full of joy and life, determined to make the best of what I had at the moment. I was an Honor Roll student, one of the top basketball players in my school, and the life of the party. Yeah, that was me!

As I sit here looking back over thirty-plus years ago, I am wondering how I missed it. How could everything so right go so wrong? It was not supposed to be this way; I was supposed to love hard, laugh loud and enjoy the time of my life, but that's not exactly how things went. Right smack dab in the middle of my thirteenth year of life, Satan planted a seed in me with the motive to destroy me. I did not know it then, but I know it now. That little thirteen-year-old girl was robbed of everything she hoped for. Everything she dreamed. Everything she believed to be. All in a moment; gone.

You see, I dreamed of going to the WNBA, and once I had my time there; my heart's desire was to be a State Trooper, funny huh? Yeah, but I had dreams back then. I hoped for a better tomorrow. I dreamed proudly, but something happened that changed everything.

One day I did as I would normally do. I went out to play football with the fellas because that is what we did. The girls, we got down with the boys, and we played basketball, football, soccer, baseball, and volleyball. Yeah, you name it, and if it involved a ball, we did it. I loved it. I loved the competition and the engagement of the game. It brought me some of my greatest joys in life to challenge and to be challenged.

Now I was called a tomboy in my day. If you as a girl did what the boys did, and you did not play with baby dolls, you were a tomboy. You didn't have tea parties, or you didn't spend time in the house cleaning, cooking, and doing what we know girls to do; you were called a tomboy. I proudly embraced it because I always challenge myself to go beyond the norm to be something other than what men would label me as. Oh yeah! It was exciting. It was fun. It was great.

Again, I say it was the best time of my life, but back to the story...

So, there I was playing football with a couple of the guys and one of them got an idea that we were to go back to his place because his parents were not home. We would have a snack, get something to drink, and we would hit the field again. Well, hey, it was not out of the norm. This was what we did. We would always hang out and go to each other's home. Normally, our parents were not there. They were always working, but we would go, sit, chill, eat, power up, and hit the field again like any other normal day.

On this fateful day, nothing about it was normal. That was the day I lost everything. It was the day I died. The day my dreams died. The day my hope died. The day my joy died. The day my peace died, that day was not a normal day. Looking back at it, I wish that day never existed. I wish it was removed entirely from the history of time.

Deal With It: The Spirit Of Anger

We were there, and suddenly one of the guys began to whisper to the other guys. My homegirl and I were there, and it began to look and feel crazy because that was out of the norm. One of them walked away to the bedroom, and we thought nothing of it. Then suddenly, the three other guys grabbed me. They pulled me to the bedroom and pinned me down while the other guy raped me. I screamed, but there was no one there to hear me. You see, my homegirl ran and left me; she did not fight for me. I was alone screaming. He was experienced, but I was not. I was innocent. I had never even thought of it. At that moment, life as I knew it was ripped from me.

It was the excruciating pain of loss. The kind of pain that a mother feels when she undergoes a miscarriage. It wasn't the bleeding or the cramping. It was the absence of hope, dreams, and a future. I had lost something far more valuable than my virginity. I felt as if I had lost my tomorrow.

Therein lies the birth of my anger, where the seed of the Spirit of Anger was conceived. I walked away from that moment bitter, ashamed, enraged, confused, hurting, and reserved. I knew I could not tell my father, and if I had told my mother, she would have told him, so I had to be reserved. I could not show signs of what I felt. I could not cry like I needed to cry; I could not vent like I would have liked to. There was no room for a release. I had to keep it bottled up inside of me. I could not let it go in fear of what would happen if I did. So, I went home, and I got myself together, and I told myself, Nori do not tell anyone. I told myself this will go away. I told myself that tomorrow will be a new day. I imprisoned myself in my pain.

Well, tomorrow came, and there I was walking down the sidewalk at our high school, and there were my friends, the guys that I played football with. The guys I hung out with every day for the past seven years of my life. There they were, laughing, pointing, and reciting my screams. As I looked up at the young man who had violated me, I saw him with a white T-shirt on with large bright red spots of blood all over it and on his shoulder. He was carrying around that bloodstain shirt as a trophy. Throughout the day, I witnessed him proudly carry that T-shirt as a claim to bragging rights against the girl that no one else could break. One thing I can truly agree with, I was broken:

my strength, my tenacity, my fight, my drive, my faith, my hope, my dreams…. they were broken.

Oh, the rage that was quickly taking hold of me. I was losing myself more and more by the minute. Somehow, I kept telling myself this will all be over soon, and things will go back to the way they once were. I kept saying to myself, "Nori, tomorrow is coming, and it will not be this way." But every day the tomorrows came, I grew worse. I kept hoping tomorrow would come, and I'd looked forward to them continuing to come in hopes that I'd get better. The pain grew deeper and deeper by the day.

John 10:10 (KJV) tells us, *"The thief cometh not, but for to steal, and to kill, and to destroy: I am come that they might have life, and that they might have it more abundantly."*

Can you see it? Can you see how The Spirit of Anger entered in through a traumatic event and began to deepen its roots? It did not care about my age, dreams, or future. It was on an assignment to destroy me.

I would spend hours upon hours staring at the ceiling or with my face to the wall as if my life had taken on some form of timeout. For months I was absent from life, simply numb. Nothing mattered; I was totally disengaged. I remember one day at basketball practice, we were doing passing drills, but something was wrong. I could not get the rhythm; my hand and eye coordination were off. I tried dribbling, but I kept losing control of the ball. I tried rebounding, but my response time was off. The trauma had caused a greater impact than I thought. For the first time, I would be benched. After getting the news, I ran to the locker room and screamed to the top of my lungs. Basketball was an outlet for me and to be benched was a grave injustice.

For weeks I sat idly by and watched my school's basketball teams soar higher and higher as I seemed to sink lower and lower. I watched how the young man who had violated me start every game; I observed his excitement and constant achievements. It seemed like life had not stopped for him at all. He appeared happier than ever. As time went by, I began to suffer severely in my academics; I went from an Honor Roll student to a D student and averaged one trip to the Dean's office a week. I had grown resentful. My attitude had taken a turn for the worst, but this would be just the beginning of my troubles.

One day a close guy friend of mine was walking me to math class. As we got to the door of the class, he inadvertently hit me on my butt, and I snapped. He still bears the scars on his face today from my uncontrollable outburst. He never spoke to me again. Another time I saw a boy pin this girl up against the wall with his hands around her neck, and I snapped. Let's just say I took on another personality toward the opposite sex. The out-of-school suspensions began to get out of hand. I fought at the bus stop, in the band room, in the cafeteria, at practice, and fought at home. It seemed as if I felt the overpowering need to always defend myself and others. Fighting became an outlet for me. The older guys in our community (School dropouts) would teach me fighting techniques. I wanted to master fighting as a coping mechanism.

Over time I would grow to master the art of cursing, lying, stealing, and manipulation. Things just seemed to only get darker for me. By the age of sixteen, I entered in and out of sexual relationships with only one goal in mind. I wanted them to hurt like I was hurting. So, I paraded as the perfect girlfriend for a few weeks only to break their heart. I distinctly remember this one young man who called my home over 15 times a day every day because I no longer wanted to have anything to do with him. Then there was a young man whose parents were friends to the family; he would come over to our home every day asking if I would come outside. I did not know how to have a normal friendship with a guy anymore, so I would always decline. But one day, I guess he had enough of me brushing him off, so he decided he would confront me as we walked home from the bus stop. The confrontation led me to a bad place in my head, I saw my attacker's face instead of his, and I went at him with everything in me. The Spirit of Anger brought an unusual yet scary strength that I would later learn to use to my advantage. This behavior would continue well into my senior year, five years later.

    By my senior year, I was totally out of control. My parents moved me to a vocational school because things were only getting worse for me. Then I found out that I was pregnant from someone I had no intentions of loving or even long-term dating, for that

Deal With It: The Spirit Of Anger

matter. My unaddressed issues of anger had complete control of my life. I continued to make one bad choice after another. Thankfully, I graduated from high school.

These issues would only continue to grow worse as I entered adulthood; I met a man I would later find out was a drug addict and womanizer. Now I was in for the fight of my life. That unhealthy relationship fueled the Spirit of Anger. His addiction caused him to say things and do things to me that were out of the norm for someone you love. I did not understand that being out of control in your life causes you to open up doors to people who, at other times, would not have access to you.

My very fellowship with this individual caused the snare for my soul. I already had my own issues, but the more I agreed with his lifestyle, the worse it got for me. You see, misery loves company. His sins feed my sins which eventually lead to a toxic explosion.

I was in a state where I was surrounded by bad company. The anger in me had driven away every good friend I ever had. I began to only attract those who had similar or worse issues than myself. We fed off of each other; we made each other worse. Sad to say, there is truly strength in numbers.

My anger eventually landed me before the judge facing 25 years to life; this would serve as the climax of my anger. That day standing before the judge served as a wake-up call for me. Regardless of the circumstances that got me there, I needed that wake-up call. I had previously offered every excuse I could possibly offer as to why I was the way I was. But at that moment, no excuse was sufficient. It was time for me to regain control of my life.

After this encounter, I began to isolate myself. I started to disassociate myself from all bad company.

CHAPTER TWO
THE SPIRIT OF ANGER

As humans, we all experience anger at different moments in our lives, which could take a toll on our health, career, and relationship if not properly managed.

Anger as a fleeting annoyance or some full-fledged and ravaging rage is absolutely normal. It only becomes a problem when it is left to go out of control when you let it get the best of you. Numerous problems result from allowing the Spirit of Anger to dominate. Invariably, the consequences permeate into the body and soul, too.

To be candid, dealing with the demon could be difficult. The secular world would suggest diverse means of getting your anger in check, but if its spirit is left unchecked, the effort(s) might be to no avail. Dealing with anger is easier if and when you can tell why and what exactly you are angry about. Usually, people feel irritable because of being deprived of sleep, stress, among other things. I mean, there is always a specific reason for being angry. Many who are aware of the tall demon they are fighting have realized that they need to seek help, especially in reducing the pain and subsiding the negative mood.

Being angry is an indication of something. But you can eliminate the anger triggers and fix the problems discovered if you would admit that anger is a spirit that must be conquered.

In James 1:19 (KJV), the Bible gave this swift instruction that "*wherefore, my beloved brethren, let every man be swift to hear, slow to speak, slow to wrath.*"

The Bible holds records of individuals who allowed the Spirit of Anger to rule their lives. The consequences are there. Moses was a prophet of God. He was robbed the fortune of entering Canaan because, "*So Moses' anger became hot, and he cast the tablets out of his hands and broke them at the foot of the mountain*" Exodus 32:19 (KJV). What took him 40 days to receive before God was ruined in a few seconds.

The rage of anger has undoubtedly torn homes, relationships, and lives apart. As an act produced out of provocation, the lessons on anger management are requisite to thriving and leading a life of purpose as believers. Perhaps the narratives would have been better if Moses had known that uncontrolled anger leaves its carrier with nothing. It robs people of their joy, peace, and dreams.

Anger is a natural and healthy emotion. Anger is motivated by sin. When you allow the Spirit of Anger to take charge, you are giving the devil a chance. When anger is used in oppression, destruction, humiliation, and impatience, destruction is imminent. It is a time bomb that explodes when ticked. The Bible says you are a fool if you allow anger. "*Do not hasten in your spirit to be angry, for anger rests in the bosom of fools.*"- Ecclesiastes 7:9 (KJV). Anger, rage, or deep-seated displeasure are not healthy to your stance as a believer. It contradicts your confession as a follower of Christ, too.

We see another example of this in Genesis with Cain and Abel. Cain's life because of anger was a contradiction to his confession and his presentation to God. Over time, Cain brought some of the fruits of the soil as an offering to the Lord. Abel also brought an offering—fat portions from some of the firstborn of his flock. The Lord looked with favor on Abel and his offering, but he did not favor Cain and his offering.

Cain became angry, and his face was downcast. Then the Lord said to Cain, *"Why are you angry? Why is your face downcast? If you do what is right, will you not be accepted? But if you do not do what is right, sin is crouching at your door; it desires to have you, but you must rule over it."* Now Cain said to his brother Abel, *"Let's go out to the field." While they were in the field, Cain attacked his brother Abel and killed him"* Genesis 4:3-8 (NIV).

Uncontrollable anger is a sin that lies at the door of many. It would behoove us to rule over our emotions of anger. Failing to do so result in a sin that will eventually control our lives. Cain was so angry with God that it produced murder in his heart. Cain ended up killing his own brother. This is a prime example of James 3:16, which states, *"For where envying and strife is, there is confusion and every evil work."*

The Lord told Cain that sin was crouching at his door. Sin was waiting to pounce on him as a lion crouches to pounce on his prey. The Lord went on to say, *"it desires to have you."* I believe this means that Satan wants to overtake us; sin wants to rule in our lives. Lastly, Cain was warned to RULE OVER IT. To rule over means to exercise complete authority over it. In other words, we need to govern our emotions. We need to govern our anger so that it does not control us.

As we can see, Cain did not heed the warning of the Lord. He invited his brother out to the field, and he allowed the sin of anger to fester and dictate his actions. I honestly believe that it confused him because of the strife that existed in Cain, and he could not rightfully decipher between righteous thoughts and evil thoughts. The evil in Cains's heart prevailed.

It's possible to become so in rage that you literally lose consciousness of what is right. This is a terrible case of anger that must not be overlooked. Evil works of all sorts start to manifest at this point. It led Cain to murder.

Irrespective of your status, personality, or title, if the Spirit of Anger dwells in you, it will follow you wherever you go until you decide to let it go. An angry believer and one who gets provoked easily needs help. Overcoming the Spirit of Anger is the key. Some practical ways to go by this are: learning to forgive people quickly, doing away with every form of bitterness, taking solace in the Word of God, desisting from judging people, and loving your neighbors as yourself. These efforts will ultimately guarantee that you live a life of peace, joy, and the absence of any shades of bitterness.

God, in His magnanimity, has made way for you in His mercies. He is aware that anger that is not dealt with can destroy you, disrupt your plan, and ultimately leave you susceptible to be pounced on by Satan. He had to do something. He sent his son to take the burdens, and with the Spirit of God, we can now boldly overcome the Spirit of Anger.

CHAPTER THREE
HOW TO IDENTIFY IT

Anger is the invisible monster that cannot be hidden. No matter how hard you try to conceal the manifestations of your anger, it just keeps seeping through. No one wants to confess to being possessed by the Spirit of Anger, and they do not have to. Anger is one of those things that show up and tell on you whether you want it to or not. Though we would like to defend and justify IT, we must identify and acknowledge it to **Deal With It**. Recognizing the cause of anger in your life is a significant step toward being free from this destructive monster.

For most people, such as myself, it was easy to identify where the Spirit of Anger first entered my life. Without a shadow of a doubt, I knew that things changed for me at the age of 13. I had a full understanding of the door the Spirit of Anger used to enter into my life. However, the task became addressing the trauma that the little girl experienced. Rape became the doorway to the Spirit of Anger, and the Spirit of Anger became the doorway for rage. James

3:16 says it best, *"For where envy and strife is, there is confusion and every evil work."* Every evil work truly sums it up for me. The trauma of rape was the initial door that Satan used to unleash hell in my life.

I understand that some try to identify the Spirit of Anger. It gets a little harder because it could be generational or progressive from many traumatic events. I want to encourage you, whether it is generational or a result of several traumatic events in your life. Your freedom is essential to a happy and prosperous life.

An angry spirit is one deprived of or lacking the necessary sanity and soundness of mind. Anger emanates from the soul. There is a constant dialogue going on in everybody's soul, and you are responsible for being able to recognize the speaker. That is how you can get to know whether it is true or not. The devil likes it when you are angry and hot-tempered. He knows he can easily attack and feed you with his plentiful deceits. As a believer, you should be able to identify when the Spirit of Anger is thriving. It is a ploy of the forces of darkness to put you in bondage and take your freedom away from you.

Deal With It: The Spirit Of Anger

The Spirit of Anger clouds your ability to think straight, correctly, and truly. You probably have heard that things are settled in the spirit realm before they're actually manifested in the physical world. Anger can affect you from the inside, outside, and through diverse means. Irrespective of the source or dimension, the sole purpose is to distract your mind, your ability to obey God's words, and consequently, your relationship with God and how to perform his ordinances to lead a well-meaning life. In essence, anger is evidenced by an inner struggle with wrath. After all, it is hard to hide. Therefore, it is easy to know and see a person struggling with unresolved wrath and anger. He or she will be easily irritable, impatient, raise their voices in a loud and harsh manner, use hurtful words, demonstrate attitudes of superiority, and put extra force into simple actions.

Ephesians 4: 31-32, however, admonishes us; *"Let all bitterness, and wrath, and anger, and clamor, and evil speaking, be put away from you, with all malice: and be ye kind one to another, tenderhearted, forgiving one another, even as God for Christ's sake hath forgiven you."*

It is pretty simple and straightforward. Once you notice that you are fast losing the grip and hold on your mind, it is a sign that the enemy – the spirit of anger - is gradually finding its way in.

Anger is a product of the desires of our hearts. James reminds us in James 4:1 (KJV),

"From whence come wars and fightings among you? come they not hence, even of your lusts that warn in your members?"

Because every hearts desire is uniquely developed, you usually would anticipate the manifestations to be unique. In Genesis 39, we find a record of Jacob's favor over Joseph and over the rest of his sons as what led to his resentment and eventual sale into slavery. You will generally know that the Spirit of Anger is alive and operating optimally when you demonstrate sinful attitudes and actions, including pride, generalizations or judging, expectations, envy, and taking up offenses.

Here is another clue: the stronger the anger or rage, the higher the pain and guilt from past experiences. Hence, we should always try to take a moment or two to reflect on things or people in past years that have gotten on our nerves and from which we are battling suppressed anger.

There are so many people who are still living in denial of the Spirit of Anger even though the signs are truly visible. Your denial of something does not make it go away as we would often think it does.

Here is a list of visible signs to the Spirit of Anger:

Irritability

Anger causes a person to become irritated with situations and circumstances that would not bother him otherwise.

Impatience

Anger reduces tolerance for the weaknesses and limitations of others. An angry person often demands an instant response to his instructions. He becomes upset if his instructions are not understood and applied.

Raised Voice

Angry impatience is usually expressed by a harsh, loud voice.

Glaring Eyes

Anger affects the facial features and empowers a penetrating glare, pronounced frown, furrowed brows, tense facial muscles, flushed complexion, prominent veins, and enlarged pupils.

Hurtful Words

An angry heart will spew out unkind words of complaint, hatred, ridicule, and rejection.

Explosive Actions

Anger puts extra force into simple actions like closing a door or setting something down. Haphazardly throwing things or pushing things around often indicates unresolved anger.

Relational Breakdown

An angry person will usually close his heart to those who offend or hurt him. This rejection is demonstrated by silence, poor eye contact, or avoidance.

Attitudes of Superiority

Wounded pride can stir up contentious anger that motivates a person to challenge others' opinions, ideas, or instructions, especially those in authority.

Physical Tension

Anger causes the jaw muscles to tighten, which brings great pressure on the teeth when they come together and leads to clenching or grinding one's teeth. Anger also causes a more rapid heartbeat, thus requiring more oxygen through heavy breathing. Anger's release of adrenaline causes the heart to pump faster and veins to become enlarged.

(Evidence of Anger signals of an inner struggle with wrath by Institute in Basic Life Principles)

In the book "*Defeating Strongholds of the Mind,*" Rebecca Greenwood talks about fits of rage.

Rebecca states, "Fits of rage are marked by explosive anger that flames into violent words or deeds." She goes on to list questions for personal assessment. To further help you identify the Spirit of

NORI MOORE

Anger in your life, I think it's important to share some of these assessment questions Rebecca has listed.

- Do you yell, scream, or throw or break things to intimidate others so that you can get your way?
- Do you angrily threaten your spouse with divorce to keep the upper hand?
- Do you typically make threats and give ultimatums when engaging in disagreements?
- Do anger and rage surface quickly when you are in a confrontational conversation?
- Do you get angry with yourself and speak harsh words about yourself out loud?
- During times of anger and rage, do you lose control and harm others? In these times, do you take personal responsibility and apologize, or do you blame the other person for your actions?

CHAPTER FOUR
ANGER IN THE HOME

"Be ye angry, and sin not: let not the sun go down upon your wrath: Neither give place to the devil." Ephesians 4:26-27(KJV)

With so much happening in the world, the home is known as our safe haven. Home is where we let our guard down and be vulnerable. It is also the place where we are the realest. The place where we are no longer wearing a mask as we often do consciously or unconsciously for the world. Home should always be the place where our strongest support system lies, the place where we have the most peace and tranquility. When we think of home, we think of family, love, unity, and rest.

I remember working sixteen-hour shifts. Sixteen hours are long for anyone but especially long if you are pulling a nightshift in a prison. These were some of the worst times of my eighteen-year career as a correctional officer. For much of my shift, I was watching the inmates in their temporary home environment. I had to keep constant watch over them as they ate, showered, relaxed, and slept, all while I longed to be doing the very same thing in my own home. I'd imagine myself home resting and reading books from my favorite authors or planning out dinner, even organizing things in my head. I'd find myself calling home to see what my husband and the kids were up to, and in some way, me staying in touch with home through my imagination or a phone call helped me get through the night. There is just something about home that makes everything alright.

We long to be surrounded by the people we love and know who loves us. We've cultivated an atmosphere of comfort through pets, pictures, furniture, devices, food, and all the other things that make us happy. There is a lot of work invested into our homes' atmosphere because it's where we spend the most time for the most part of our days. Home is where the heart is!

Unfortunately for many, this just isn't the case. As lovely and peaceful as a home should be, it doesn't always go this way. Especially when the Spirit of Anger

Deal With It: The Spirit Of Anger

is in play in your home. It doesn't matter who it is. The spirit is operating whenever the Spirit of Anger is in operation; there is no peace, comfort, or joy. It seems like everything that is supposed to be, we are simply robbed of by the Spirit of Anger. Having our emotions in control doesn't just help us, but it also helps the people around us.

Being able to handle situations proportionately and peacefully like Christ would, without blowing things up or stuffing your feelings, is a commandment. It can be the distinguishing factor between you and the rest of your folks, friends, and relatives. A Christian home where either or both spouses allow the Spirit of Anger is heading towards destruction. Psychologists believe that unexpressed anger has a bad impact on communication.

I can remember growing up having friends whose close family members dealt with anger. I literally hated going to their homes. It seems like everybody was always mad about something. When there was no reason to be angry, it seems like anger was always on the scene. It seemed as if someone was always frustrated and agitated and out of control about something.

Anger infuses fear in the home. Whenever anger is in play, someone is afraid. Often, we do not realize how malicious the Spirit of Anger is and how it literally dominates our environment. Can you imagine wanting to laugh, wanting to share the excitement of your day, and being gripped by so much fear that you feel like you cannot rejoice like you need to? I have been there. I've literally been in that place where I felt like my greatest moments had to be suppressed because of what was in the atmosphere because the Spirit of Anger was in control.

The Spirit of Anger doesn't just rob the carrier, but it also robs those who live in the same environment.

In many cases, arguments escalate because of what one party thinks is being said and not always because of what is actually said. This is what we find in many homes. Perhaps this explains why people resort to practicing passive anger. Unfortunately, there are assumptions that by ignoring anger or pretending not to be angry, couples can avoid potential problems. This is not true. Unexpressed anger piles up and accumulates to become a tremendous force of resentment.

The impact of anger on health is also destructive too. Anger, being more than a feeling, can result in health problems. Increased levels of anxiety, shortened lifespan, heart disease, weakened immune system, and increased risk for stroke and heart attack are possible consequences of breeding anger in your home. What exactly did Jesus preach and command us to do? To love our neighbors as ourselves. But an angry person cannot love. This is the catch: inability to control anger in the home can produce unimaginable and horrible consequences- leaving the door for the devil to work his way confidently into Christian homes and destroy them.

To hear my kids tell the story of a younger me breaks my heart. As my kids were growing up, I dealt with the Spirit of Anger strongly in my life. As I have previously shared with you, being raped at the age of thirteen caused my life to go on a downward spiral. Demonic doors were opened, and sin sat in. This was no easy fix. I suffered for years, even through the upbringing of my children. It was not until my children were adults that they felt comfortable sharing certain stages of them with me. They were literally traumatized throughout most of their childhood by the monster that lived vicariously in me. Looking back, I can recall times when I must admit I was out of control. I remember when my son's teacher called, and they were having an issue with him at school. Well, I'm the type of person that wants to hear both sides of the story. I listened to the teacher, and I listened to my son's side of the story without thinking; I unconsciously grew angry. I was literally at the point of boiling over to learn the details of the incident.

My son often looks back at that moment and tells me how embarrassed he was by how I exploded. You see, I always thought that I was taking up for them, and I vowed no one would take advantage of them, no one would mishandle or mistreat them in any type of way, and so in my mind, I would fight for them tooth and nail as long as they were right. In any way, they had received injustice; I was going to deal with the matter strongly.

Deal With It: The Spirit Of Anger

The truth of the matter is, I was not fighting for them; I was fighting for me. The little girl in me was crying out. The little girl in me was fighting to defend herself. As I look back on my children's lives, I realize that I was reliving my childhood all over again.

It didn't just stop there, there were times when my children would break something very expensive, or they would damage something in the house. They had to master hiding things from me because they did not want to become a victim of my anger. I can now identify how my children lived in fear of the monster growing inside of me every day. It is a hurtful feeling to look back at my children's lives, and as much as I love them and as much as I did for them and supported them, to know they lived in fear. I can often remember my oldest son telling my younger sons to hush because you will make Mama mad. So certain things that happened to them in school, they would not share with me. I didn't get to become a part of certain things they experienced in life; the Spirit of Anger robbed me of a true relationship with my children. My children love me and honor me, but to know that they feared me is heartbreaking.

Often we desire to ignore what is actually happening on the inside of us; we easily overlook it and move on as if we're the only one who has to deal with the monster that is raging on the inside of us. We are not the only ones suffering. Our spouses are suffering, our children are suffering, our parents are suffering, anyone and everyone connected to us is suffering at the hand of the monster that we refuse to kill. Unexplainable nights of unrest exist in homes every day as a result of the Spirit of Anger.

Anger is also a direct result of violence in the home. CDC places anger management issues at the top of the list as to why abuse exists in the home. One out of four women and one out of seven men will experience violence in the home daily. The National Statistics says that 20 people per minute or physically abused on a typical day have more than 20,000 phone calls placed due to some form of violence. Anger isn't always the issue, but most of the time, it is the dominating factor in the situation.

I love Ephesians 4:26-27(KJV), *"Be ye angry, and sin not: let not the sun go down upon your wrath: Neither give place to the devil."* It carries within it a powerful key to dealing with anger. We were never told not to be angry because anger is s natural emotion. However, we are instructed not to allow the sun to go down upon your wrath; in doing so, the seed of the adversary that feeds anger sets in and grows in our hearts. It festers within us, and we grow worse by the day.

What differentiates anger as a mere and normal emotion or sin is largely dependent on how you deal with it as a person. Therefore, the husband must learn to control his emotions and anger as much as the wife. Apart from this being an indication of discipline, you can win and overcome the spirit with prayer and thoughtful practice. First, identify what makes you angry. Then proceed to determine how God would want you to react. Fill the vacuum by engaging yourself in something you enjoy doing and following what the scriptures say about anger.

Determine to seek God's face in prayers. Admit that you are helpless and that only God can help you control it. "*I desire then that in every place the men should pray, lifting holy hands without anger or quarreling.*" I Timothy 2:8 (KJV). You cannot be two things at the same time: an angry spouse and a prayer warrior. You see why it is important to deal with the Spirit of Anger? Otherwise, it steals and robs you of the peace and joy you enjoy in His presence.

Apostle Paul writes in *Corinthians 10:5* that we should take every thought captive into the obedience of Christ before it becomes a stronghold in our mind. You do have a choice to make - to continually fuel your emotions of anger with the wrong thoughts or decide to take a stand with God and rely on his help to help you keep the situation in check.

Learn to say "No!" to the feelings and thoughts that are likely to upset you before they get the better of you. *"You have heard that it was said to those of old, "You shall not murder; and whoever murders will be liable to judgment." But I say to you that everyone who is angry with his brother will be liable to judgment; whoever insults his brother will be liable to the council; and whoever says, "You fool!" will be liable to the hell of fire* (Matt. 5:21–26)?

Here, Christ expands on one of the ten commandments, emphasizing that there is more in this context than mere murder and that anger and insults are prohibited. Anger is egregious and should not be found in a Christian home.

CHAPTER FIVE
ANGER IN THE WORKPLACE

"Let all bitterness, and wrath, and anger, and clamor, and evil speaking, be put away from you, with all malice" Ephesians 4:31

Dealing with anger as a Christian would allow you to see how you measure up against the fruits of the spirit specified in Galatians 5:20-21 "*The fruit of the Spirit is love, joy, peace, longsuffering, gentleness, goodness, faith, meekness, temperance.*"

In fact, the Bible does not even recognize anger as the last action or response to the worst of life's circumstances. Therefore, you are expected to be a peacemaker and solution-provider, one who takes control of your emotions. This is further reiterated in Paul's message to the church in Colossians that, "*But now you must also rid yourselves of all such things as these: anger, rage, malice, slander, and filthy language from your lips.*" Colossians 3:8 (KJV). Indeed, these vices are destructive and vicious because they do not edify the Gospel of Christ. It begins from home, and even at your place of work, anger is usually a revelation of the factors that are going on in our lives. Thus, it can be a helpful warning light that should be given prior attention.

Anger in the workplace is often the result of unresolved issues, negative thoughts, and/or feelings that have been lodged in your heart and are consistently and negatively impacting your day. Failure to address the issue at hand only results in bitterness and resentment and ultimately vicious episodes of rage.

Whether you are harboring your feelings for not getting the promotion, being overlooked for a major project, being mishandled, or inappropriately addressed by your superior. All these things can cause major issues in the workplace if they are not dealt with quickly. Most times, we resort to saying things that we really do not mean. Still, because we have suppressed our feelings and emotions for so long, we often explode by saying things that cannot be taken back. Anger often leads to making irrational decisions on your job or uncontrollable vicious actions being displayed by you due to what you have been feeling for so long.

Anger in the workplace creates a toxic environment. Anything toxic causing unpleasant feelings can be harmful and even malicious in nature. A toxic environment is any place or any behavior that causes harm to your health, happiness, and wellbeing. Working around people who always make you feel inferior, insecure, or unworthy suggests the presence of a toxic environment. When there is a consistent presence of emotional pressure that causes you to feel afraid, embarrassed, or livid, there is a strong possibility you are working in a toxic environment.

The workplace naturally comes with various stress levels; it is up to us to manage those stress levels that we engage in daily. I worked in a high-level security prison for over eighteen years. It was a stressful environment that I had to learn to manage for my overall sanity. There were days I improperly managed those levels of stress, and as a result, my anger got the best of me. I quickly learned that things would spiral out of control whenever I failed to properly steward my emotions. We can never control the overall environment of the workplace, but we can control ourselves. When it comes to anger, we must learn to properly rule over our emotions.

And the Lord said to Cain, *"Why are you so angry? And why do you look annoyed? If you do well [believing Me and doing what is acceptable and pleasing to Me], will you not be accepted? And if you do not do well [but ignore My instruction], sin crouches at your door; its desire is for you [to overpower you], but you must master it"* Genesis 4:6-7 (AMP).

To say the least, exhibiting prolonged anger at a colleague, coworker or employer may be a strong indication that something is not right in your life. It could seem to people as though you feel threatened-real or imagined. You are being humiliated or lack control over your situation and the different life circumstances.

King Solomon writes in Proverbs 11:19, *"A man's discretion makes him slow to anger, and it is his glory to overlook a transgression."*

Simply put, a balanced life validates a sense of discretion. It is a sign of wisdom to handle these perceived transgressions. Your ability to demonstrate slowness to anger is a mark of strength and leadership. This can make you stay employed longer than a wrathful person. No one enjoys working with an angry person. They are considered and seen as toxic.

We normally spend anywhere from eight to sixteen hours in the workplace. That's 40 to 80 hours a week under high levels of direct or indirect stress. Suppose we do not learn to effectively manage the stress in our work environment. In that case, it can and will eventually take a toll on our physical health. Stress is not good for anyone over long periods; it eats away at our vital organs. It literally breaks us down from the inside out. I remember throughout my 18-year tenure as a correction officer, I suffered from high blood pressure, migraine headaches, and unusual discomfort in my body. All these things were a direct result of the high levels of stress I consistently engage with daily. Over time I developed improper eating habits, disturbed sleep patterns, and severe weight gain.

The job itself was not stressful. It was the unmanaged emotions of the people who carried out the job. All these individuals who failed to effectively manage their emotions created a toxic working environment. The environment was harmful to the individual, but it became harmful and destructive to everyone who operated in the environment. I often found myself saying this job is so easy it should never be this stressful. Still, whenever there is disunity, discord, or strife on any level, it produces such an aggressive environment.

  I quickly noticed how I had begun to burn through my sick leave. I went to doctor's visits after doctor's visits only to learn that there was nothing that the doctors could actually do for me other than medicate my symptoms. I realized that if I want it to truly be healed in this area, I must learn to responsibly manage my stress. It had to begin with me. First off, I had to be honest with myself; I had to face the hard issues that I had suppressed for so long. One of the first things that I started to do was be honest with myself and be honest with others.

  If I was offended, I'd let them know that I was offended. I never left the situation as it was; I always sought out a peaceful conclusion to the matter. In doing this, I found that I walked away every day feeling better about myself and my job. This was so important for me. I had been harboring ill feelings for so long because I felt mishandled or overlooked at times. Sitting down with my supervisors and expressing myself, and getting to voice how I saw things gave me a satisfying level of relief. It literally removed the tension from my work environment.

The second thing that I started to do was begin each day with a positive affirmation I spoke positive words over myself, over my position, over my coworkers, and my supervisors. Positivity drives out negativity. That was it; I needed to drive out all negativity within my work environment. I had to be intentional in this place if I genuinely wanted to see change.

It was essential for me to forgive. It was hard to revisit this area, but I needed to forgive everyone who had offended me, everyone, who had wronged me, and everyone who felt like I was inferior to them. I had to forgive them and see them from a different perspective. I postured my mind to find the positive side of every individual and focus on that positive regardless of how great the negatives may have been. I made the positives my daily focus. As I consistently did this, I noticed my heart, feelings, and thoughts toward my work environment began to change for the better.

Certainly, I needed to improve the communication. For so long, I had focused on just minding my own business and staying in my own lane. Working in such a toxic work environment causes you to literally shut down. When we shut down, we fail to communicate the proper information needed to effectively make the overall goal flow; 70% of business mistakes result from poor communication. (©2021 Delta Quest Media) So, I was as much a part of the problem as others. When we shut down, it literally brings stagnation and delays to everyone in the workplace. Communication is a major key. Proper communication not only motivates the employee but also lifts the overall morale in the workplace. Where the morale is high, there is less likely to be a toxic environment. Through time I was able to see how communication began to drive out misunderstandings in the workplace. I also learned that a lot of my anger or aggression from my workplace was due to a misunderstanding. So, I made it my business to learn how to accurately convey information to my team.

Deal With It: The Spirit Of Anger

Through proper communication, I learned how to effectively set boundaries and how to properly give recognition.

Overall, I believe it's safe to say that I began to identify the areas I was enraged about. I began to correct these things within myself. I began to make the necessary changes. It started with me, and as I began to change things within myself, I began to see my work environment shift according to the change that I started.

Do you work with angry people, or do you at least know why they are angry? Now, can you deal with them? Yes, I agree that the workplace is an environment that could spur provocations and feelings of anger, among its consequences. Poorly managed anger can take a toll on the productivity of the organization, among other negative impacts. The cost can also be devastating. Hence, the onus is on you to conduct your due diligence by keeping your emotions in check and working on dealing with your anger.

CHAPTER SIX

ANGER IN RELATIONSHIPS

"Do not even associate with a man given to angry outbursts. Or go [along] with a hot-tempered man" Proverbs 22:24 (AMP).

Anger is an uninteresting part of our personal, political, and cultural rhetoric. The usual representation of anger in the scriptures is God's rage against sin. He detests sin because it offends his personality as a righteous God. Sin also corrupts the creation of God, as well as rebels against his sovereignty. This is a typical example of anger in relationships- and it is never a pleasant experience when the Lord reveals His anger against men. In this case, anger becomes the appropriate response to a human's effort to suppress the truth, continue to dwell in immorality, and reject His will.

Even at that, the Bible says in Psalm 103:8-11, that *"The Lord is merciful and gracious; slow to anger and to abound in steadfast love. He will not always chide, nor will he keep his anger forever. He does not deal with us according to our sins nor repay us according to our iniquities. For as high as the heavens are above the earth, so great is his steadfast love toward those who fear him."*

Although God would ensure that His justice is satisfied, He always provides an escape for His people. It even got better when He sent Jesus to satisfy the demands of Godly justice and to ensure that going forward, the wrath of God will not fall on those who trust Jesus. This is exactly the same kind of relationship we all should have with others- one which spares judgment or justice but particularly seeks and strives to love irrespective of the condition and circumstance. As much as the Lord himself has been patient with us even in our sin, it becomes expedient that we extend similar kindness to those who sin against or offend us. In addition, you should strive to control your emotions and make sure your anger does not drive your actions. Many times, if you do not, you may end up regretting this.

There are four different types of relationships: Family relationships, Friendships, Acquaintances, and Romantic relationships.

In our family, some are blood-related to us or connected to us by way of marriage. We cannot choose our biological family. This is one relationship that has been predestined from the beginning of time. Although the family relationship was pre-determined, we have the choice to decide the value of the relationship. We have the right to decide if we want to develop a relationship with a family member or not. For example, a father may choose to remove himself from the life of his son. Though the father and son are biologically related, the relationship no longer exists at the father's decision. There are many family relationships today that are nonexistent because of a choice that someone made. Regardless of what makes you family, each relationship must be a healthy one. Healthy relationships are the building blocks to teaching us how to have stronger relationships in other areas of our life.

Friendships are created with people that we have grown to love and trust outside of the family. Friendships are built over time as two people grow to know each other; they establish a loyalty system through mutual respect. Normally these two people will have common ground that draws them together, ultimately determining how close a friend they eventually become.

On the other hand, acquaintances do not fit in the family or the friendship category; however, there are some common interests involved. You may communicate or even fellowship with acquaintances frequently. Still, they just do not fit in the category of a friend. A colleague is a great example of an acquaintance; they are often around. There is a level of mutual respect and common ground. However, they are not considered a friend.

Then there is the romantic relationship when two people take their friendship to another level. Normally in a romantic relationship, two people are sexually involved with one another. Romantic relationships are not only seen between husband and wife. It can also be seen between a male and a female companion or same-sex companions. It is important to know that as we look at the word romantic in relationships, it strongly influences love.

Regardless of what type of relationship it is, there are a few things that must be present. There must be a connection, mutual respect, honesty, loyalty, and love in some respects in a relationship. When all these elements or most of these elements are present, you will see the forming of a beautiful relationship.

Proverbs 22:24 Warns us not to associate ourselves with a man given to anger or aggressive outbursts and not even go along with the hot-tempered individual. This is especially important when forming relationships; often, we focus on honesty and loyalty, common ground, and even their ability to aid us in the direction we desire to go. One of the things that we do not look at as we are developing relationships is the character in a person; this is incredibly important in any formed relationship. An individual's personality speaks loudly. Their personality must be compatible with your personality to establish a wholesome relationship, whether romantic or working.

The purpose of dealing with anger in your relationship with coworkers, friends, relatives, or other persons in society is balancing the response of anger to the injustice we seek about things done to you and the wrongness in yourself.

Sin corrupts our perceptions about people and things, and so does anger. It impairs your ability to make wise and reasonable decisions. This is bolstered in Psalms 37:8, "*cease from anger, and forsake wrath: fret not thyself in any wise to do evil.*" You will be doing yourself and people you love a great favor by taking time to respond or react to actions or inactions that could prompt you to pour some rage on them. The best time to make decisions is when you are certain that your anger is no longer clouding your judgment of things and people.

Another thing to be wary of is the anger of others. You do not want to make friends with a wrathful man. In the same way, no one likes to deal with you if you are seen as a wrathful person. Anger is contagious, and you can become more prone to it if you live around it too much. But if anger is already a big deal and a struggle for you, you have to watch out for your mental, physical and spiritual wellbeing.

The scripture tells us to avoid angry men and not to befriend them or associate ourselves with them in any way. Through studying the Word of God, we learn that angry men are fools. If we want a peaceful life, it will behoove us not to enter into such relationships.

First Corinthians 15:33 says, *"evil communication corrupts good manners,"* to understand this, you must understand that you will be tempted to learn the habits of angry men, which will, in turn, cause you immeasurable times of trouble. Anger truly does rest in the bosoms of a fool. They glory in their anger because they are enslaved to it. Having a relationship with men who are enslaved to anger causes a snare to your soul. As mentioned, it is equally important that we are not the friend who is trapping others' souls.

Indeed, every relationship is constituted by imperfect people, who generally often have varying expectations. Therefore, it is not strange to find that people get disappointed because they expect things to be great at all times. Couples having disagreements in a relationship is absolutely normal. And while many couples have it at the back of their minds that they will not always agree with each other, many fail to understand that anger in their relationship is dangerous. Anger in relationships will inevitably cause irreparable damage. It is easy to continue to be angry when the other party angrily deals with you, resulting in further escalation.

Uncontrolled anger results in physical, emotional, or verbal abuse; meanwhile, we must understand that no form of abuse should be tolerated in a relationship.

CHAPTER SEVEN
ANGER IN MY CALLING

"I will bless the LORD, who hath given me counsel: my reins also instruct me in the night seasons." Psalms 16:7

I am a dreamer; I have been a dreamer since as far back as I can remember. Throughout my life, God has been dealing with me through dreams and visions. It was through a dream I choose my career path. It was through a dream the man I would marry was confirmed. It was through a dream I understood my call to ministry. I have grown to understand that God is serious when I receive a series of dreams alluding to the same message; it's urgent and immediate action is required on my part. This has been one of my strongest ways of communication and guidance since I was a little girl. The Lord has given me counsel, correction, and prophetic words for myself and others by way of dreams.

Deal With It: The Spirit Of Anger

  Through my struggle with the Spirit of Anger, The Lord has given me insight and strategic ways to eradicate the ruthless monster called anger and its counterparts from each area of my life. It required me trusting solely in him and obeying him to the letter. Many days, I cried because of what he would allow me to see in operation within me. I tried denying it, but the dreams would only get stronger. He was revealing areas in my life where I thought I did an awesome job of masking, escaping, or ignoring the Spirit of Anger.

  One night the Lord gave me a dream of my leaders at the time. In the dream, he showed me that they would call me with accusations against my integrity. This was a tough area for me because I had suffered severely in this area before. I had almost lost my mind. Well, the dream revealed I would be tried in this area yet again. In the dream, I received the call, and at the hearing of their words, I began to boil-over with anger. The very memory of what I had previously suffered and the thought of suffering to that degree over again resulted in me becoming unhinged.

  As I viewed my response in the dream, I began to cry out to God for help. I was seeing a side of me I thought I was beyond. I had tried hard to get better, be forgiving, be patient, and kind to others even when they were not to me, but this dream clearly showed I had not made the progress I assumed. As the dream continued to play out, I distinctly remember praying for help. I acknowledged that I was not strong enough to deal with the Spirit of Anger that ran deep in my life. I knew I needed help, something far beyond the natural; I needed supernatural intervention in my life—the type of intervention that could only come from God above.

    After I woke up, I went into prayer. I was shaken by what I saw. I was afraid that it will come to pass, and yet again, I would return to the place I have been fighting to be freed from. This dream brought a determination to demolish the very existence of this monster once and for all. It was not as simple as I thought it would be. I needed a strategy; I needed to be fervent in my approach. With the guidance of the Holy Spirit, I devised a plan. Sure, enough the call came just as the Lord had shown me in my dream. This time, I was ready and armed. I was not unaware of Satan's devices; they would not work or prevail this time.

Deal With It: The Spirit Of Anger

As I sat on the phone listening to the heart of my leaders as they raised accusations against my integrity, I began to breathe slowly yet deeply. You see, in times past, I would rear out of control, but I needed to control myself. I needed to master controlling my own spirit if I would hope to prevail. So, I was slow to respond; I listened well. Then when it came to my time to respond. I opened my mouth, and to my surprise, my words were guided by the Spirit of God. The conversation went so well. I was not angry, outraged, or agitated; I was at peace. Whew! What a victory. I finally prevailed in a place I have been consistently defeated in for years.

Medical experts claim that anger is a natural phenomenon, positing that anyone would get angry at a perceived threat, especially against their position or wellbeing. Although these health professionals are equally wary of the danger of keeping anger suppressed or pent up, they recommended that it is better to express the feelings via reasonable discussion or to engage in a healing activity.

Galatians 5:20-21, however, says, "*the fruit of the spirit is love, joy, peace, longsuffering, gentleness, goodness, faith, meekness, temperance."* Anger, therefore, clearly contradicts this commandment. Therefore, to exhibit anger as a general and common response is acting in contradiction to the fruit of the spirit.

As a minister of the Gospel who leads people of God while administering the scriptures to them regularly, you are not automatically absolved of feeling or getting angry. We find many "men of God" flare-up at events or situations when triggered and begin to question their stance in God or their acclaimed salvation. Anger and its feelings are sinful and undue, but if you are ever in the position of leading or bringing God's people to the kingdom- as a pastor, preacher, evangelist, or what have you, you must learn to, and prayerfully seek the fruits of the spirit. The worst thing you can do is lose your temper before your destiny helpers. Losing your temper with those sent to help causes your helpers to walk away, and doors closed on you.

This is one of the ways to curb the feeling when the situation arises. Of course, no two people manage their anger the same way but growing and watering the fruits of the spirit, among other things such as seeking

Deal With It: The Spirit Of Anger

Christian counseling and suppressing the feeling, will go a long way in dealing with it. One difficult aspect of anger is letting it go. Be deliberate about tolerating human differences and be willing to forgive anything, the same way your role model- Jesus Christ- would. That way, you can overcome the Spirit of Anger in your calling and ultimately perform your calling more effectively.

I have learned to count the little victories if I hoped for total victory. The Spirit of Anger was an enemy to my soul. It constantly warred against the righteousness of God in my life. Every private failure will show up publicly if it goes unchallenged in our lives.

I remember when I served as a Prophet of God in the Lord's church, yet I strongly battled with the Spirit of Anger. One day my son came home from the church's daycare upset that one of the teachers had put her hands on him in an aggressive way. As I listened to his side of the story, I could feel the rage welling up inside of me. I could hardly wait till the next day to confront the teacher. The next day I stormed into the church's daycare seeking to defend my son. I had lost all reasoning. I wanted to rip that teacher to shreds. I was out of it, literally out of it. Everyone saw the rage in me and quickly began to clear a path. Right before I reached her, I heard in the distance behind me, "Is that the Prophetess?"

They could not believe what they were seeing because I had done so well to mask it. It went unchecked privately, and so it was able to overthrow me publicly. This was one of the most humiliating moments I've had as a minister of God. My true nature was exposed so everyone could see that I had been walking only in the form of godliness, but I had truly denied the true power of God in my own life. Had I acknowledged His true power, the works of the flesh would have surely been defeated within me. There I was, a phony, unable to live the very words I preached.

Often the Lord will allow great times of exposure when you have consistently ignored his warnings privately. Man, did this wake me up? We are good with an evil being present in our lives if no one else knows. This exposure pushed me to face what I had run for so long in my life. My secret was out, I was not Ms. Perfect, but I had an uncontrollable sin raging in my

Deal With It: The Spirit Of Anger

life. The powers of darkness had a hold on me, and at the slight bit of agitation, it would rear its ugly head.

I could no longer ignore this sin in my life. The dreams began to now come with scriptures. I could hear myself quoting them in my sleep. *"Be ye angry, and sin not: let not the sun go down upon your wrath"* (Ephesians 4:26), *"And the servant of the Lord must not strive but be gentle unto all me"* (2 timothy 2:24), *"He that hath no rule over his own spirit is like a city that broken down and without walls"* (Proverbs 25:28).

As the series of dreams kept coming, so did the scriptures. I would learn to war with the Word of God over my life. God meant business, and I had ignored this hideous monster long enough.

Unknown to me, I had preached through the Spirit of Anger, conducted church meetings, and even prayed through the Spirit of Anger. How do I know? The series of dreams were all about me. They were actual times in my life where IT had taken complete control of me. God was taking me back in time to show me my folly. I was being challenged to get it right. Repent and turn from that course of action forever. This was not an easy process for me. There was a true breaking of pride in play in my life, and I had to be mature enough to surrender.

I remember a service the Lord told me in a dream He wanted me to attend. There would be a lot of seasoned leaders there. He said to me, "Nori, I want you to go and openly repent before the people. It must not be a general apology but rend your heart before the people in true remorse for your immaturity in ministry." This would be one of the hardest tests yet. I had strongly believed in my heart that I was innocent before those leaders, but God saw otherwise. I wrestled with God all night till early the next morning. Finally, I broke. I had been charged by God to complete a task, and I understood from previous experiences it would be foolish to fight against God.

So, I went and did just as the Lord instructed me, and boy was I glad I did. Years of hurt and bitterness broke off me. I was set free in so many ways I truly cannot tell it all. Let's just say my life and ministry took quantum leaps in the spirit and has so ever since. You see, God never uses anger to fulfill His purposes.

CHAPTER EIGHT
ANGER IN ABSENCE

In times of great stress or adversity, it's always best to keep busy to plow your anger and your energy into something positive.
-Lee Iacocca

How much more grievous are the consequences of anger than the causes of it. **-Marcus Aurelius**

There is an anger that arrives from the pain of absence. The absence of a loved one is the result of death or separation; you feel its pain. If not effectively managed, it can become overwhelming to you.

Loss creates a void in us that can only heal through time. Loss is defined as the state or feeling of grief when deprived of someone or something you value. Grief is a natural response to loss. The pain of unmanaged grief grips your life and imprisons you. Feelings of hopelessness, helplessness, disbelief, guilt, abandonment, and even anger began to quickly overtake you. Grief becomes the stronghold of your mind, unwilling to allow reason.

Anger is a normal reaction often accompanied by denial, depression, and loneliness. This is especially true when dealing with death. Often you are angry because you feel like you have been robbed. You begin to lash out and blame others. We must be mindful not to hurt the ones we love, or it will only cost us more loss.

I remember the day my grandmother died; it was one of the worst days of my life. I had a special relationship with her where I could share anything with her, free of judgment. Losing such a dear friend and loved one who made a major impact on my life was devastating. Many of us have suffered loss at the hand of death. Some we have overcome, and some have we have not. Grieving is an imperative process with any loss. However, the important thing is to not allow grief to overtake us. I remember blaming the doctors, even blaming my mother for not taking proper care of her. None of these things were true. It just felt better to blame others than to come to the reality that it was her time.

We must allow ourselves to feel and embrace the absence.

Grieving is often associated with death; however, any loss/absence can cause some form of grief. Whether it is the loss of a job, a pet, a dream, a friendship, foreclosure to a home, or a divorce. It is quite natural for us to grieve in some manner in the absence of anything or anyone we valued.

We live in a society where little girls and boys grow up in single-parent homes far too frequently. They spend most of their lives suffering from the Spirit of Abandonment and the Spirit of Rejection. They are grieving the absence of a parent. Often they take on guilt, and they literally wear themselves out by believing that it's their fault because their father/mother isn't there. They began to blame themselves for their family falling apart. So they spend their life trying to fix something they didn't break because they feel responsible.

Guilt is an emotional state where we experience conflict at having done something that we believe we should not have done (or have not done something we believe we should have done). This can give rise to a feeling which does not go away easily and can be difficult to endure ("Dealing with Feelings of Guilt" Diana Lalor @ Cottesloe Counseling Center).

In any case of absence, identifying the significance of what/who is absent is the beginning of our healing process. Regardless of the onset of grief, we must seek out healthy ways to deal with the absence. Seek out methods that, in time, can soothe your sadness and aid you with coming to terms with your loss/absence.

CHAPTER NINE
ANGER AND ME

"A [shortsighted] fool always loses his temper and displays his anger, But a wise man [uses self-control and] holds it back." Proverbs 29:11 (AMP)

Throughout my learning journey to deal with the Spirit of Anger, I knew I lacked self-control. I failed to rule over my natural emotion of anger. My inability to do so eventually grew into a rage, a rage that scared even me. Rage is seen as a wave of violent and uncontrollable anger. It bears no warning signs. I have experienced many lows due to my inability to maintain self-control. Anger always damages those around us, but the most damage is done to the individual who possesses the Spirit of Anger. Anger became the aggressive destroyer in my life, destroying my hopes and dreams, relationships, great opportunities, and ultimately destroying me spiritually.

Under the influence of the Spirit of Anger, we can never see how great the damage is in our lives. Most often, we don't even realize the damage done, not just to us but to those around us. Anger became an aggressive destroyer in my life, destroying everything I put my hands to. This was a vicious monster! My lack of discipline in this area spiraled out of control. I didn't know it then, but I definitely understand it now. Anger is a natural emotion that must be governed. Governing the Spirit of Anger is not an easy task. It is something that we must work diligently at for the overall peace and sanity of our lives. Fighting against this spirit was not just for me but for those I loved. It was for my goals and my dreams.

There was a time in my career where I desired to move up the ranks. I did everything necessary to ensure my advancement; I worked long hours, studied hard, and was mentored by the best in my field. I failed to understand that even though I had done all of these things, one thing that I had not been diligent about would be my demise. I was considered most likely to succeed and promote to the next level until that dreadful day came. To become a supervisor, I had to have great conflict resolution skills; after all, I worked in a confrontational environment. It was the one skill that I should have naturally possessed. It had happened so many times in my life until I just became numb to it. And just like that, my dreams were crushed; I would no longer be considered for promotion.

The destructive power of anger cannot be overemphasized. One person would say the way they react to tough situations is dependent on how angry they are at that present moment. But is that the most we can do as humans and, secondly, as believers?

Anytime you get angry, and whatever approach you adopt to deal with it, the focal point of concern is how you feel at the end of the day. The effect on your psychological self is as important as on your spiritual being. Demonstrating anger will get you nothing. It does no good to you, neither does it solve your problems. It can destroy everything you seek or desire in life- both physically and emotionally. More so, it has a way of demolishing your mental peace because an angry person usually feels frustrated, exhausted, and sad at the end.

Anger is responsible for the bulk of the changes we experience in our brains, including hormonal activation and the response, bringing about shouting and throwing things. When you get angry, many things, including your arterial tension, heart rate, and testosterone production, increase—unfortunately, the cortisol level decreases, leading to anxiety, depression, or irritability.

Generally, anger makes you a different person than you should be. It causes you to do strange things that you may end up regretting. That reminds me of the famous quote, *"controlling your mind and anger can make you the king of your own."*

As Christians, getting angry is something we have to be wary of, regardless of the situation. We only are better at controlling the short fuse than others. Ungodly anger can ruin jobs, friendships, and relationships. The Scriptures tells us, *"For the wrath of man worketh not the righteousness of God."* James 1:20 (KJV). This is an instruction to do away with and manage anger and its various causes. You should strive to lead and live a peaceful life. That way, we can avoid the damnation of the effect. Some biblical tips can help us understand the power of anger as an emotion.

The appropriate response to anger would be to set your will to forgive, demonstrate lovingkindness, exude calmness, and practice non-attachments from diverse situations at all times.

CHAPTER TEN
HOW TO HEAL ANGER

I believe anger is the commonest of the various emotions we experience in our lives. Everyone gets angry, and most of us do it passionately- which makes it horrifying. If you have been dealing with anger for some time, it probably has sparked your curiosity about why it happens so often. You want to be a peaceful and loving person, but anger gets the best of you. Considering the two levels of anger- the deep suppressed type which almost everyone has to an extent. If this type of anger remains unaddressed and remediated, it can destroy. The reason is simple: the mind controls the body, and suppressed anger will in little or no time begin to manifest as diseases. Suppose you get into conflict easily and are likely battling suppressed anger from different experiences. In that case, you need to seek help, and yes, you can get healing.

Also, there is the type of anger that I consider absolutely necessary - the type we should not run away from when the feelings come knocking, the type of anger which we experience in our day-to-day activities, the type of anger that could get out of hand if you are battling suppressed anger from past experiences. Only a thin line exists between differentiating this type of anger as the healer and the destroyer.

Talk to God to heal you absolutely from the Spirit of Anger. He will listen and hear you. He will help you and save you from being crushed. Although things may not happen as rapidly or quickly as you expect. Apostle Paul assures us, "*Likewise the Spirit also helpeth our infirmities: for we know not what we should pray for as we ought: but the Spirit itself maketh intercession for us with groanings which cannot be uttered*" Romans 8:26 (KJV).

Giving in, surrendering it all to God, and seeking help through the spirit will ensure that you can deal with anger in the long run. You will then enjoy a life of absolute peace.

Not only that, if you should see a therapist or psychologist, please do. They have the required years of experience and expertise to help and guide you in dealing with it (anger) as a person. Again, what works for one person may not be suitable for another. This is the more reason you should understand yourself and see what works best for you.

I would strongly recommend the Word of God as a powerful tool in driving out the Spirit of Anger. Counseling is good; however, I personally found conversations that I was unwilling to have with anyone, professional or not. In these times, it was the Word of God that got me through.

I would research scriptures decreeing and declaring them over my life. I spent countless hours meditating on the Word of God, even praying it. In the book of Hebrews Chapter 4:12, I read that God's Word is quick and powerful and sharper than any two-edged sword piercing even to the dividing asunder of soul and spirit and of the joints and marrow and is a discerner of thoughts and intents of the heart.

As I read this verse of scripture, I thought, wow, this is what I need. I need something that can operate, energize, and effectively cut between the soul and the spirit all at the same time. The Word of God gets down to the deepest part of our nature, exposing and judging every thought and intent of our heart. This process produced healing in unexplainable ways in my life. Again everyone is different, and knowing yourself will help you determine what method is best for you. One thing we know for sure, action must be taken. You can no longer stay as you are and expect to heal.

My Personal Journey of Healing

It is important to note that my journey is not complete and to be perfectly honest, I will always be a work in progress. I am truly grateful that I am not where I once was. This journey of healing is taking place under the hand of God himself. I am so grateful for my friends, family, counselors, mentors, and ministry companions. They all played a role in helping me get to where I needed to be. But for me, ultimately, at the end of the day, I had to get before God and allow the Word of God to perform surgery on me.

This has been a very long and tedious journey. However tedious my present journey is, I am so grateful that I took the leap in healing myself. My prayer is today that as you have been reading this book, you're being ignited. I pray, through encouragement, you would have the faith you need to begin your journey of healing from the Spirit of Anger.

Let me explain why I said that my healing journey is taking place under God's hands. As I mentioned previously, I am a dreamer. The Lord speaks to me through dreams and how forever grateful am I that God would lead me personally in this manner. After years of continual defeat at the hands of the Spirit of Anger, the Lord began to give me dreams regarding the Spirit of Anger deeply rooted within me. I knew that God wanted me to do something about it. These dreams showed me a side of myself I could not see.

I was blinded to my own reality, and the Lord used the channel of dreams to reveal to me what I could not see about myself naturally. As I experienced dream after dream, I began to get a fight on the inside of me to see that monster annihilated in my life. I gained another sense of strength and tenacity to stand against the monster I had bowed to with each dream. It was truly an internal fight, but God strengthened and prepared me for the daily fight that I would have to engage in through dreams. There were days I experienced extreme mental agony, but I was determined to be victorious.

I want you to understand that my journey is not an easy one. However, I understand that I needed to overcome the Spirit of Anger. Throughout my healing process, there were times I hated myself; I had to remind myself in those moments that God loved me, and I was not alone, but God himself was fighting with me.

My healing process is not perfect. It is rugged. I have good days; I have bad days. There were days I fight well, and there were days I don't fight at all. Even throughout my healing process, I lost friends. I mishandled people, but I learned to be better; I learned to rule over the Spirit of Anger.

This healing process is teaching me the true meaning of repentance. As I previously stated in chapter "Anger In Ministry," The Lord had me in a process where I had to publicly repent to leaders. I am still learning the art of repentance and embracing it every day. God is literally healing me through my repentance.

I also learned the importance of forgiveness. I began to understand the power of unforgiveness and the effect that it had on my life. So throughout this healing process, I had to learn to forgive. One of my favorite passages of scripture that dealt with forgiveness is Luke Chapter 17, as Jesus was teaching his disciples if a man offends you and he repents, forgive him. Jesus told them if he offends you seven times a day and repents for the offense that he has caused unto you, they must continue to forgive. This is the type of forgiveness that literally wipes away all previous offenses.

If my brother trespass against thee, take heed to yourselves, rebuke him; An if he repents, forgive him. And if he trespasses against the seven times a day, and seven times in a day turn again to thee, saying, I repent; Thou shout forgive him.
Luke 17:3-4

A lot of my rage resulted from resentment and bitterness because I was not willing to forgive. So, throughout this healing process going on a mission to forgive is essential. Regardless of how often I had been offended by that same individual, I needed to wipe their slate clean. I had to literally begin to uproot resentment, which caused bitterness of soul. Resentment is bitter indignation at having been treated unfairly. Throughout this process, I've learned to properly handle the anger and disappointment at being treated unfairly.

    I'm mastering the technique of redirecting and rerouting the natural emotion of anger.

NORI MOORE

RESOURCE
SCRIPTURES & PRAYERS

2 Timothy 3:16 reads, *"All scripture is given by inspiration of God, and is profitable for doctrine, for reproof, for correction, for instruction in righteousness: That the man of God may be perfect, thoroughly furnished unto all good works."*

Being fully armed with this understanding, it will be wise for us to review the scriptures related to the Spirit of Anger. Where we lack inspiration, the word will encourage us. Where we lack wisdom, the word will provide sound doctrine, and where we lack correction, the word will give us a strong rebuke where we need to understand God's ways. The word will provide instructions unto righteousness.

I want to share the tools I use to strongly judge the Spirit of Anger in my life.

The book of Luke Chapter 4 gives an account of Jesus fasting in the wilderness for 40 days. After he fasted, Satan came to tempt him. Satan targeted three areas in Jesus' life. He said the first thing was, if you are the son of God, tell this stone to become bread Jesus answered it is written man shall not live on bread alone. Being defeated by the Word of God, Satan tried Jesus again. The Bible says that the devil let him up into a high place and showed him in an instant all the kingdoms of the world. And he said to him, I will give you all their authority and splendor. It has been given to me, and I want to give it to you; if you worship me, it would all be yours. Again responding with the Word of God, Jesus declared it is written to worship the Lord God and serve him only.

Here, Satan being unsuccessful yet again, tries Jesus for the third time. This time Satan led Jesus to Jerusalem and had him stand on the highest point of the temple. He said if you are the Son of God, throw yourself down from here. Satan now tries to overthrow Jesus with the Word of God by saying, *"it is written he will command his angels concerning you to guard you carefully they will lift you up in their hands so that you will not strike your foot against the stone."* However, Jesus is not being moved at the tactics of Satan. He answered, it is written do not put the Lord your God to the test.

Jesus used the Word of God. He continued to declare that it is written. I believe for many of you, you must use the Word of God in every area of your life where Satan is raging. Every place in you that is under siege or where you are being strongly tempted, you must resist the devil by way of the Word of God.

I want to encourage you to study, meditate, memorize, and pray the following scripture. Sometimes, it is very helpful if you study the scriptures in different translations. Find a translation that you can understand; we have provided you the scriptures in the King James Version.

"He who is slow to anger is better than the mighty, and he who rules his spirit than he who takes a city." - **Proverbs 16:32.**

-May you learn the art of being slow to anger
-May you learn to rule well over your spirit

"The thief cometh not, but for to steal, and to kill, and to destroy: I am come that they might have life, and that they might have it more abundantly." — **John 10:10**

Deal With It: The Spirit Of Anger

-May you no longer fall prey to Satans demonic agenda in your life.

-May you experience the abundant life for the rest of your god-given days.

"Wherefore, my beloved brethren, let every man be swift to hear, slow to speak, slow to wrath." —James 1:19

-May your willingness to hear and reason well increase supernaturally

-May you be slow to speak and slow to wrath

"Do not hasten in your spirit to be angry, for anger rests in the bosom of fools." -- **Ecclesiastes 7:9**

-May you forever be counted as wise and emotionally sound.

-May every foolish way be put far away from you.

"For where envying and strife is, there is confusion and every evil work." —James 3:16

-May you be loosed from the sins of envy and strife.

-May you walk in the spirit of sobriety, giving no place to evil works.

"Let all bitterness, and wrath, and anger, and clamor, and evil speaking, be put away from you, with all malice: and be kind to one another, tenderhearted, forgiving one another, even as God for Christ's sake hath forgiven you.
-***Ephesians 4:31-32***

-May you experience divine deliverance from evil works

-May you walk habitually in the love of God, fully taking on His character and attitude

"Be ye angry, and sin not: let not the sun go down upon your wrath: Neither give place to the devil.
– ***Ephesians 4:26-27***

-May your natural emotions of angry never gain an advantage over you.

Deal With It: The Spirit Of Anger

-May you never allow the sin of rage to last throughout the night.

-May Satan have no occasion in your life.

"I desire that in every place the men should pray, lifting holy hands without anger or quarreling. **– 1 Timothy 2:8**

-May the Spirit of grace and supplication overtake you

-May you have clean hands and a pure heart before the Lord

-May your worship be purified before the lord

"From whence come wars and fightings among you? Come they not hence, even of your lust that war in your members?"

-May every severe and bitter battle be put away from you

-May the root of cardinality be driven out of you

-May you learn to walk in the Spirit of God with all mankind

"You have heard that it was said to those of old, "You shall not murder; and whoever murders will be liable to judgment." But I say to you that everyone who is angry with his brother will be liable to judgment; Whenever insults his brother will be liable to the council; An whoever says, "You fool!" will be liable to the hell of fire. **– Matthew 5:21-26**

-May the scepter of Jesus touch the room of your heart and produce understanding to his instructions

-Make every murderous intent in your heart be eradicated, delivering you from the danger of the judgment

-May every feeling a passionate abhorrence be broken off of your life

-May words of vulgarness being fueled by the spirit of anger be driven out of you

"But now you must rid yourselves of all such things as these: anger, rage, malice, slander, and filthy language from your lips." **-Colossians 3:8**

-May the strength of God to put off these destructive and vicious traces of worldliness come upon you

-May you arise and put off old destructive habits And habitual sins

-May the Lord set a watch at your mouth so that you cannot sin against him

-May you set your mind on things which are above, Study them, let your heart be entirely engrossed by them.

-May you continue to walk in the union of Christ Jesus, overriding every sinful passion of old

-May the power of the Holy Spirit enables you to live in supernatural power with the ability to overcome impossible things

"Do not even associate with a man given to anger outburst. Are go along with the hot-tempered man."
-*Proverbs 22:24 AMP*

-May you completely disassociate yourself from ungodly ill-noble and ruthless men.

-May your soul never be ensured by the companion of a fool

"*Evil communication corrupts good manners; may you never be deceived in this way.*"- **1 Corinthians 15:33**

-May the Lord surround you with wise men

The fruit of the spirit is love, joy, peace, longsuffering, gentleness, goodness, faith, meekness, temperance.

– **Galatians 5:22-23**

-May the fruit of the spirit conquer the works of the flesh in your life

-May you walk in the agape love of Christ, the love that overrides the spontaneous heart and makes a conscious decision in mind. This agape love requires you to seek the highest good for another regardless of any level of insult, injury, or humiliation that you have received at the hand of man

-May the Spirit of gloom and misery be broken off of you And grant you are abiding joy that cometh not from earthly things but its foundation is God

-May you have the peace of God that is positive and feel with blessings and goodness in the absence of wars. I declare over you the peace that surpasses all understanding. A peace that ensures calmness and settling.

-May you possess the ability to bear adversity, injury, and reproach. May the patience of God be your portion as you walk and longsuffering

-May you be counted faithful before the Lord.
-May it is said of you that you are reliable even in the hardest times of testing and temptation

-May you walk in the spirit of gentleness, having the right amount of anger at the right time, never allowing the explosion of rage in your life

-May you walk in the spirit of moral excellence and kindness. May the fruit of goodness abide in you

-May you confidently trust in the Lord our God all the days of your life, producing great faith

-May you endure injury with patience and without resentment, and the spirit humility rest upon you as you walk in the fruit of meekness

-May you be self-disciplined able to control your own spirit.

CONCLUSION

The Spirit of Anger hurts the individual, family, relationship, and the larger society. It is manifested in situations where people perceive they have been rejected, hurt, offended, or violated over a word or action. Anger, being no respecter of age, culture, race, social status, or other classifications, can have devastating consequences, particularly if unresolved. Identifying its root cause would be that you are taking your life into retrospect to determine whether you have suffered the pain of rejection at some point or are only reacting to the unchangeable or uncontrollable features of your lives.

All of us are born with one need or the other but without the adequate skills to meet them. This is why we find ourselves relying on the government, family system, or other things to make ends meet. Our inability to meet these needs can get us angry, and the emotional trauma grows like wildfire over time. It even becomes worse if your situation is toxic and unpleasant in a sense. But this message of hope is for everyone who seeks help with dealing with the Spirit of Anger,

Deal With It: The Spirit Of Anger

having come to terms with the fact that it is destructive. That is not the kind of feeling you want to go on for so long. In a bid to preserve your life, relationship and be well received by God and society, it becomes extremely important that you understand the things that make you angry. Know how to deal with people who get on your nerves and find means to deal with the Spirit of Anger.

In this book, I have shown you real-life examples and practical ways to deal with anger. We can all make the world a better place by combating the Spirit of Anger!

NORI MOORE

MY REFLECTIONS

Deal With It: The Spirit Of Anger

NORI MOORE

Deal With It: The Spirit Of Anger

NORI MOORE

ABOUT THE AUTHOR
NORI MOORE

Conference speaker, revivalist, pastoral counselor, and mentor Nori Moore is a woman after God's own heart, seeking to lead the people of God by providing strategies and tools to empower the Church to be efficient in the ministry of prayer, intercession, and deliverance. She currently serves in the Body of Christ as an Apostle in The Lord's Church.

At the age of 19, Apostle Nori gave her life to the Lord under the leadership of Pastor Author L. Brown at Rosedale First Born Church. Through many trials and tribulations, she has found her purpose in the Most High God to serve his people in love and intercession. Her passion for God and surrendered lifestyle has led to an anointing to pray, preach, and teach the word of God with authority, revelation, and deliverance.

Today, Apostle Nori is the proud and devoted founder of Emmanuel Global Ministries, with locations in various cities. Using her expertise in Anger

Management and Christian Spiritual Counseling, Apostle Nori and her ministry effectively deal with the reality of Christian issues calling for true deliverance and unmasking. She develops prayer, intercessory prayer training materials, and other media to assist in providing sound teaching and guidance for the 21st-century church.

When she's not running her ministry, Apostle Nori serves the Lord as an inspirational, thought-provokingevangelical speaker, delivering messages that inspire, encourage, and bring effective change in the lives of those who embrace the word of God. She also enjoys spending quality time with her six handsome young sons in their hometown of Tallahassee, Florida.

www.ingramcontent.com/pod-product-compliance
Lightning Source LLC
Chambersburg PA
CBHW050654160426
43194CB00010B/1931

Tabla de Contenido

Evangelismo Personal..1
Prólogo..7
Capítulo 1: El Llamado al Evangelismo................................9
Capítulo 2: El Mensaje del Evangelio..................................13
Capítulo 3: El Poder y el Rol del Espíritu Santo en el Evangelismo 19
Capítulo 4: El Ejemplo de Jesús y la Iglesia Primitiva......25
Capítulo 5: Desarrollando un Corazón Ganador de Almas........33
Capítulo 6: El Poder del Testimonio Personal 39
Capítulo 7: Métodos de Evangelismo 45
Capítulo 8: Respondiendo a las Preguntas Difíciles 51
Capítulo 9: Evangelizando a Grupos Específicos 57
Capítulo 10: Evangelismo y Seguimiento Espiritual........63
Capítulo 11: Proyectos Prácticos de Alcance 69
Capítulo 12: Avivamiento y la Iglesia Evangelística 75
Capítulo 13: Qué Decir al Perdido......................................83
Capítulo 14: El Evangelista y el Espíritu Santo 91
Capítulo 15: Recompensas Eternas del Evangelista 97
Biografía del Autor – Dr. Greg Wood.............................. 107